Martin Luther King

Paintings by Malcah Zeldis

Words by Rosemary L. Bray

A Mulberry Paperback Book   New York

The full-color artwork was prepared with gouache paints on paper.
The text type is Palatino Bold.

Text copyright © 1995 by Rosemary L. Bray
Illustrations copyright © 1995 by Malcah Zeldis

The Library of Congress has cataloged the Greenwillow Books edition of *Martin
Luther King* as follows:

Bray, Rosemary L.
Martin Luther King / by Rosemary L. Bray;
pictures by Malcah Zeldis.
p. cm.
ISBN 0-688-13131-X (trade) ISBN 0-688-13132-8 (lib. bdg.)
1. King, Martin Luther, Jr., 1929–1968—Juvenile literature. 2. Afro-Americans—
Biography—Juvenile literature. 3. Civil rights workers—United States—
Biography—Juvenile literature. 4. Baptists—United States—Clergy—
Biography—Juvenile Literature. [1. King, Martin Luther, Jr., 1929–1968. 2. Civil
rights workers. 3. Clergy. 4. Civil rights movements—History. 5. Afro-
Americans—Biography.] I. Zeldis, Malcah, ill. II. Title.
E185.97.K5B73 1995 323'.092—dc20 [B]
93-41002 CIP AC

10 9 8 7 6 5 4
First Mulberry Edition, 1997
ISBN 0-688-15219-8

In memory of Morris
and Jack Brightman,
my father and brother
—M. Z.

To my beloved son,
Allen James,
and the other children
of the dream
—R. L. B.

In 1929, not long after New Year's, a son was born to Alberta King and her husband, the Reverend Michael L. King, of Atlanta, Georgia. They named their child Michael L. King, Jr. But a few years later Reverend King decided to change his name to Martin and changed his son's name as well.

The Kings were a middle-class black family living in the South of the 1930s. They had enough food and clothes, and they had a pleasant home to live in. But where they could go and what they could do were limited by segregation—a series of laws and customs that kept blacks and whites apart in many ways.

Segregation meant different things in different places. At the movies, for example, blacks sat in the shabby and uncomfortable balcony, while whites sat downstairs, in a cleaner and more attractive part of the theater. On buses black people had to sit in the back, away from white people. Whites could go out to dinner at any restaurant they chose, while most restaurants were closed to black people. The laws segregating blacks from whites differed from one part of the country to the other, too. In the South blacks and whites often lived near one another. In the North, however, blacks and whites lived in completely separate neighborhoods. But whatever the specific laws were, white people were treated better than black people.

Black people had learned to make the best of situations that were meant to hurt and insult them. Their churches were a good example. When black people first came to America, they were gradually banned from attending church and praying with whites. They formed their own churches and ordained their own ministers. They prayed and sang the way they wanted to, and they began to organize and work to improve conditions for all black people. Something that was intended to crush their spirit became instead a source of strength for them.

The Reverend Martin King was the minister of one such church—the Ebenezer Baptist Church in Atlanta. And though the times were very difficult for black people, he believed that things would be different one day, that the attitude of white people toward blacks would change. He very much wanted his son Martin Luther King, Jr., to believe that, too.

But as young Martin grew older, it became harder for him to believe that white people would ever change. He hadn't always felt this way. When he was very small, he had played every day with a little boy who lived across the street from the King family. The little boy was white, but Martin didn't think that was important.

When Martin went to school for the first time, he thought they would go together. But when he didn't see his friend all day, he went to his house to ask about him. His friend's mother told Martin that her son and he couldn't play together anymore, because her son was white and Martin was colored. "Colored" was what most people called black people in the 1930s.

Martin was very hurt. For the first time his mother had to explain to him about segregation. "No matter what the rest of the world says," she told him, "you're as good as anybody else."

It did not prevent Martin from feeling bad anyway, and he began to notice things he had not paid attention to before. He saw the way clerks treated his mother and father when they all went shopping. Sometimes the Kings waited a long time before anyone in the store would help them. Sometimes no one would help them at all. Yet when someone white came in, the clerks would answer questions and help the white customer right away.

Martin noticed that white people were sometimes angry with him just because he was around. Once a white woman slapped him on the face as they passed in a downtown store. When someone asked why she had slapped him, the woman said, "That little nigger stepped on my foot." The slap hurt Martin, but the name she called him hurt just as much.

Martin wasn't always hurt and angry. In many ways his life was pretty much the same as that of other boys his age. He fought with his little brother, A.D., and his older sister, Christine. He had a paper route. He went to school every day. Martin especially liked school. He loved giving speeches and writing compositions. When he was fourteen, he entered a contest for the best essay written about black people and the Constitution of the United States, and he won first prize.

Martin and his family were proud. So was his teacher. Together, Martin and his teacher traveled by bus when Martin went to receive his prize. On the way back to Atlanta a white man got on the bus, but there were no more seats. The driver told Martin to get up and give the white man his seat—another one of the rules of segregation. At first Martin wouldn't get up. It wasn't fair. The bus driver was furious and called Martin ugly names. Martin knew that if he kept arguing, he and his teacher would be in danger. Finally he gave up.

Martin had never been angrier in his life. How could it be that he could win a prize for writing about the rights of black people and still not even have the right to keep his seat on a bus? He tried not to hate white people after that, but it was hard.

When Martin was fifteen, he was accepted at Morehouse College in Atlanta, where his father had gone to school. Soon he was studying and thinking more than he ever had before. He decided it would be wonderful to become a professor, to study and to teach.

His father wanted him to be a minister, but Martin always said no. Then at Morehouse Martin began to change his mind. He'd always been interested in ideas, and the teachers at Morehouse made some ideas unexpectedly exciting, especially those about religion. Studying with these teachers helped Martin begin to think differently about God. Eventually he surprised his family by deciding that becoming a minister could be a good thing after all.

So Martin told his father that he wanted to study at Crozer, a school for ministers in Chester, Pennsylvania. Most of the students who went to Crozer were white. They were polite to Martin, but that was all. Still, he was excited to be living in the North. For the first time in his life he felt free.

In 1950, his last year at Crozer, Martin traveled to Philadelphia to hear a lecture by Dr. Mordecai Johnson, the president of Howard University, an important black college. Dr. Johnson was speaking about a Hindu lawyer and activist named Mohandas K. Gandhi, who had lived in India until his assassination two years earlier, in 1948.

Gandhi and his followers had fought to free the Indian people from the rule of the British in a way no one had ever fought before. Gandhi believed that love was the most powerful force in the world. He thought that if you faced your enemies with love, without violence, and insisted that they do the right thing, you could win. Many times Martin had heard his father say he should love his enemies. He'd thought that meant being weak and afraid. But Gandhi never seemed weak or afraid.

Martin read about Gandhi for years. The more he read and heard, the more he wondered: Could black people in America do what Gandhi and his followers had done in India? Though he didn't know it at the time, Martin would one day have a chance to find out.

By the time Martin finished his studies at Crozer, he had won the respect—even the friendship—of his classmates. He was graduated from Crozer at the top of his class and went on to study at Boston University to earn his Ph.D. degree. He loved all the things he was learning at the university, but he was lonely and far from home. His friends thought he should meet a young woman they knew. Her name was Coretta Scott, and she, too, was a long way from home. She had come from Marion, Alabama, to study singing at the New England Conservatory of Music.

Martin and Coretta liked each other when they met. They both were intelligent and had dreams of doing important things, and they both were angry about the way black people in America were treated. Martin asked Coretta to marry him as soon as she was graduated. It was a hard choice for Coretta. In those days women who married usually gave up their own work to help their husbands, and she wanted very much to be a singer. But she loved Martin, and she believed in his work. Martin and Coretta were married in 1953.

Martin and Coretta remained in Boston for another year. They loved the North and wanted to stay. Martin planned to teach while he completed his Ph.D., and he was offered jobs at several colleges. He was also asked to be the pastor of a church in Montgomery, Alabama. The Dexter Avenue Baptist Church had heard about Martin and asked the Kings to visit. Coretta wasn't sure she wanted to live in her home state. But they found they liked the church and the people, and agreed to move in 1954.

The year 1954 was a very important one. The Supreme Court of the United States decided that sending black children and white children to separate schools was unconstitutional, that this violated the fundamental rights of all Americans. Many people believed the decision, called *Brown* v. *Board of Education of Topeka, Kansas,* was the first step toward the end of segregation in America. Now it seemed that changing the old ways just might be possible.

They were right. The old ways were going to change. And Martin Luther King, Jr., would be the person who did the most to make those changes. He began his work in Montgomery the very next year, with the help of a woman named Rosa Parks.

Rosa Parks worked in a Montgomery department store and rode the bus home from work every day. On December 1, 1955, the bus she was riding got crowded; soon white people were standing in the aisle. The driver stopped the bus and told the people in the first row of the colored section to give up their seats—but Rosa Parks didn't. Her feet hurt; she was tired. It wasn't fair, so she refused. The driver said he would call the police. Mrs. Parks told him to do so. The police said they would arrest her if she didn't get up. She told them to go ahead and arrest her. In jail Mrs. Parks decided to fight.

osa Parks got help from the National Association for the Advancement of Colored People (NAACP). The head of the Montgomery NAACP, Edward Nixon, helped her get out on bail. But the NAACP did not stop there. Mr. Nixon suggested they stage a one-day protest in the form of a bus boycott. For one day—the day Mrs. Parks was going to court—black people were to refuse to ride any bus in Montgomery. He called Martin and asked if he would help. Martin said he would be glad to do what he could, and Mr. Nixon told him that he had already volunteered the Dexter Avenue Church as a place for people to meet to plan the boycott.

By the time the meeting ended that night, everyone had been assigned a job. A group of women printed up thousands of leaflets and distributed them all over town. Ministers of all the black churches in the city talked about the boycott during their services. People called their friends and neighbors, urging them not to ride the buses.

Still, no one was sure if the boycott would work. No one had ever tried to do such a thing in Montgomery. And most black people didn't have cars. If they didn't ride the buses, how would they get to work? Martin worried that some people might lose their jobs. There was nothing to do but wait and see.

The next morning Martin and Coretta got up and looked out their front windows. They lived near a bus stop, and they wanted to see how many people would be riding. The first bus came—and it was empty! The second bus came—and it was empty, too. All over Montgomery black people walked or rode in private cars—or stayed home.

The boycott lasted for an entire year. At first white residents of Montgomery ignored the protest. They figured that black people would get tired of walking and use the buses again. But they didn't. The ministers who had helped organize the protest formed a group called the Montgomery Improvement Association (MIA). They elected Martin president. When he talked about how important the boycott was, even people who were afraid of losing their jobs or being attacked listened.

The Montgomery bus company was losing a lot of money, but it wouldn't change its mind. Citizens who didn't like the boycott harassed the protesters. And people began to threaten Martin, Coretta, and their baby daughter, Yolanda. One night someone bombed the house they lived in. Luckily nobody was hurt. The MIA sued the bus company and the city so that black people could sit wherever they pleased on Montgomery buses. Finally, on December 20, 1956, the court ruled in favor of the protesters. To most people who had followed the boycott, it seemed like a miracle.

The success of the boycott made Martin famous, and the book he wrote about it, *Stride Toward Freedom*, made him even better known. Schools all over the country offered him jobs as a teacher and speaker. Once upon a time he would have been thrilled to take a teaching job. But he had learned he could help his people more by inspiring them to organize and stand up for their rights.

In 1957 he met in New Orleans with hundreds of ministers from black churches all over America. They formed an organization called the Southern Christian Leadership Conference (SCLC). Its purpose was to encourage churches and religious groups to work for the rights of black people. The ministers named Martin president of the group.

Martin and Coretta knew it would take a lot of power to free black people, and that power, they believed, had to be based on love, on nonviolence. They knew one reason the Montgomery boycott had worked was that the protesters had used nonviolence as their weapon. The black men and women of Montgomery had not fought physically with the bus company. They had simply refused to accept being mistreated.

What the protesters did—their civil disobedience—had been inspired in part by Mohandas Gandhi and his struggle for the freedom of the Indian people. Now people who had worked with Gandhi before his death asked Martin and Coretta to visit their country. When Martin returned to America, he was more than ever convinced that even though Gandhi's religion was different from his, both religions believed that love, not violence, was their most powerful weapon.

Martin continued to work for the freedom of black people, and throughout the United States others were beginning to join the cause. More and more people believed the time was near when black Americans would be granted the civil rights they deserved as citizens of the United States, the rights other Americans took for granted. And even people who didn't agree had begun to pay attention to the growing numbers of those who were willing to protest against segregation.

By 1960 Martin was so busy organizing SCLC that he thought it was time to leave the Dexter Avenue Baptist Church. He decided to return to his hometown, Atlanta, and to his father's church, Ebenezer Baptist. He planned to work part-time and spend the rest of the time helping people throughout the South to organize.

One day in February 1960 four black college students in Greensboro, North Carolina, walked into a Woolworth's store to have lunch. They sat down at the lunch counter, but the waitress refused to serve them. The students said they would not leave until she did. Soon others from the school, North Carolina Agricultural and Technical College, joined them. The students were arrested, but the sit-ins didn't stop. They spread.

Before long students from all over the country were traveling to southern towns and being arrested in protests like the one in Greensboro. Martin decided to join them. When students held a sit-in at a restaurant in an Atlanta department store in October 1960, Martin Luther King, Jr., was arrested along with them.

The students were soon let go. But a judge sentenced Martin to prison, and he was sent to one of the most dangerous jails in the South. His family and friends were afraid that someone would hurt him or even kill him there. But Senator John F. Kennedy (who was elected president a month later) helped get him out of jail. It was the senator's brother Robert Kennedy who asked the Georgia judge to let Martin go free.

That wasn't the last time Martin went to jail. He continued to believe in civil disobedience, in the idea that it was better to go to jail for breaking an unjust law than to give in to that law, and he continued to encourage others to disobey the laws that treated black people unfairly. He hoped the police would fill the jails with protesters. Then everyone would know how unjust many of the laws were.

In 1963 Martin Luther King and the SCLC decided to work in Birmingham, Alabama, where Martin's brother, A.D., lived. Birmingham was one of the worst places in the country for black people. The police commissioner, a man everyone called Bull Connor, believed strongly in segregation. When the SCLC protests began in April, Connor and his men arrested hundreds of people. The police were so brutal and the opposition so fierce that protesters feared for their jobs and their lives.

At one meeting it was suggested that college students who joined the sit-ins be asked to march so they would be arrested. Flyers were printed asking students to come to a meeting. On the night of the meeting not just college students came. Kids from high schools and even from elementary schools joined them. Freedom was as important to them as it was to their parents. At first some people worried that the children might get hurt. But others believed that growing up with segregation would hurt them even more. Finally it was decided that anyone eight years old and over could participate in the march planned by the protest organizers.

On May 2, 1963, almost a thousand children joined what some called the Children's Crusade, a march from the Sixteenth Street Baptist Church into the center of Birmingham. The entire city was shocked. The police were too surprised to do anything.

People all over the country were shocked as well. Each night films of the protesters were being shown on the television news. Each morning pictures of the marchers appeared in the newspapers. No one had expected that children would actually participate. Many of the marchers returned the next day. But this time the police came with their dogs, and the fire department came with their hoses. Connor ordered his men to stop the march. The water from the fire hoses knocked down men, women, and children. The dogs bit them and chased them.

When people all over the country turned on their televisions that night, they watched the police abusing black citizens simply because they wanted the same rights as everyone else. And many people who had never thought about civil rights before began to think about them.

That summer Martin and other civil rights leaders organized a march that would be bigger than any previous one. They wanted people from all over the country to go to Washington, DC, and demand equal rights for black Americans. People of every race and color who believed in justice were asked to join the March on Washington on August 28, 1963.

More than 250,000 people came. Standing in front of the Lincoln Memorial, Martin Luther King, Jr., gave what has become one of the most famous speeches in the history of America. He talked about his dreams for the United States and his hope that all people would one day be able to live together in peace. People cheered and cried when they heard him. It was a speech that became known all over the world.

Still, there were people who hated the very principles Dr. King and others believed in. A few weeks after his speech a black church in Birmingham was bombed. The bomb killed four black girls, ages eight and nine, as they were changing into their choir robes. Most people couldn't believe what had happened. But Martin knew that some people opposed civil rights for black people enough to kill—even to kill little girls. Knowing that didn't make it easier for him. More than ever, Martin believed that violence was never the answer. But it seemed that violence was everywhere.

On November 22, 1963, President John F. Kennedy was assassinated. Martin had worked and talked with the president many times. They hadn't always agreed on the best way for black people to win their rights as citizens, but they had agreed the day would come. Now the president was dead, and Martin worried more and more that violence would take over as the way for humans to deal with one another.

In December 1964, when he was thirty-five, Martin Luther King was awarded the Nobel Peace Prize in recognition of all he had done for civil rights and nonviolence. He was the youngest person ever to receive the prize.

But there was still much work to be done, and whenever he could, Martin answered the calls for help. One such call came from Selma, Alabama. In January 1965 Martin and other members of his group announced they planned to go to Selma to organize a voter registration drive. More than 370,000 black people who were eligible to vote in Alabama had not registered. People who tried to register were turned away, even threatened. Martin wanted to change that.

Day after day black people marched to the courthouse in Selma to register. During the first march police chased them. The police shocked some with cattle prods and beat others. One young man was killed. Later a minister who had come was beaten to death by three men. Though terrible things were happening, Martin knew the registration drive had to be continued. He decided to lead a march from Selma to Montgomery, fifty miles away, where his fight for freedom had begun. By the time the procession arrived in Montgomery five days later, thirty thousand people had joined it.

Martin hoped to meet with the governor of Alabama, George Wallace, but the governor refused to talk to him. It didn't matter. The march made its point. People all over the country saw how determined the marchers were, and President Lyndon Johnson had already agreed to support a law that would protect everyone's right to vote. That law, the Voting Rights Act, was passed later that year.

Martin began to turn his attention to the northern states and the conditions that black people faced there. School and housing restrictions, for example, were different from those in the South. Martin moved his protest campaign to Chicago to draw attention to the problems that urban black people lived with every day.

He also began to speak out against the United States involvement in the Vietnam conflict. Martin thought the U.S. presence in Vietnam was immoral, and he made speeches saying so. Many people who had admired him were now angry with him for disagreeing with the government. They said he should stick to the civil rights issue.

Martin replied that he was a citizen of the world and that he cared about all people. As a minister he had a responsibility to speak out against violence wherever it occurred, and nothing, he believed, was more violent than an unfair war.

By 1968 Martin and his followers had begun to think more about all the poor people in the United States. Poor people of every race and color, he believed, had many of the same problems and the same dreams and should work together to improve their lives. Martin thought a Poor People's March, similar to the 1963 March on Washington, would be a good idea. Not everybody agreed with him. It was much harder to organize such a protest, harder to get both people and money for it. Many were tired of marching. Nevertheless, Martin believed that the example of poor people organizing to fight for a better life would be an inspiration to others.

In Memphis, Tennessee, a group of sanitation workers were going on strike. Martin agreed to march with them through the streets of the city on March 28. It was supposed to be a peaceful march. But a neighborhood youth gang thought nonviolence was a waste of time and decided to disrupt the march. They broke store windows and fought with the police. One of the gang members died.

Many people blamed the violence on Martin. Martin, however, tracked down members of the gang and talked with them. They were surprised that someone as famous as he would take the time to meet with them. They agreed to support the next march, scheduled for April 5, and promised Martin that it would be peaceful.

They never had a chance to keep their promise. On April 4, 1968, Martin was standing on a balcony outside his hotel room. Several of his close friends who were inside the room heard a popping noise. They looked out onto the balcony and saw Martin lying on the ground, bleeding. He had been shot.

Martin Luther King, Jr., died an hour later at a Memphis hospital. He was thirty-nine years old.

All over the world people were hurt and angry. There was rioting across the United States. Martin's wife, Coretta, pleaded with people to stop the violence. She knew it would have been the last thing her husband would have wanted. Men and women from every country sent letters and tributes to Martin's life and work. They wanted Americans to know that Martin Luther King, Jr., was someone they would never forget.

There were Americans who believed that Martin deserved a national holiday. They believed it would be the most suitable way to honor the man who had done so much to change the way black and white Americans viewed one another. Old enemies of Dr. King didn't want to see him honored, but in 1983 the U.S. government declared January 15, Martin Luther King, Jr.'s birthday, a national holiday.

Today, in every country in which people value freedom, there are those who read and study the work and writings of Martin Luther King, Jr., a black American who became a citizen of the world.

The Life of
Martin Luther King, Jr.

January 15, 1929	Born in Atlanta, Georgia.
June 1948	Receives B.A. degree from Morehouse College in Atlanta.
June 1951	Receives B.A. degree from Crozer Theological Seminary in Chester, Pennsylvania.
June 1953	Marries Coretta Scott in Marion, Alabama.
September 1954	Becomes minister at Dexter Avenue Baptist Church in Montgomery, Alabama.
May 1955	Receives Ph.D. from Boston University.
December 1955	Helps to organize a bus boycott in Montgomery to protest segregated buses; becomes head of the Montgomery Improvement Association.
December 1956	Boycott ends when Montgomery bus company agrees to desegregate buses.
August 1957	Becomes president of the Southern Christian Leadership Conference.
September 1958	*Stride Toward Freedom* published.
February 1959	Visits India with Coretta to study nonviolent tactics of Mohandas Gandhi.
January 1960	Becomes co-pastor of Ebenezer Baptist Church in Atlanta.
October 1960	Arrested at a sit-in in Atlanta.
December 1961	Arrested at a prayer vigil in Albany, Georgia.
October 1962	Meets with President John F. Kennedy to discuss civil rights.
April 1963	Arrested during protests in Birmingham, Alabama; writes *Letter from a Birmingham Jail* while imprisoned.
August 1963	Gives "I Have a Dream" speech at the March on Washington.
December 1964	Awarded Nobel Peace Prize.
March 1965	Organizes voter registration march from Selma to Montgomery, Alabama.
August 1965	Voting Rights Act signed by President Lyndon B. Johnson.
August 1965	Makes his first public statement against Vietnam War at SCLC conference.
March 1967	Continues opposition to Vietnam War in Chicago speech.
March 1968	Leads protest of sanitation workers in Memphis, Tennessee.
April 4, 1968	Killed by a sniper at the Lorraine Motel in Memphis.
November 1983	An act of Congress designates the third Monday in January as a legal holiday celebrating the birth of Martin Luther King, Jr.